Last will and best guesses

poems by

Deborah Jang

Finishing Line Press
Georgetown, Kentucky

Last will and best guesses

for Mark

Copyright © 2022 by Deborah Jang
ISBN 978-1-64662-977-0 First Edition
All rights reserved under International and Pan-American Copyright Conventions. No part of this book may be reproduced in any manner whatsoever without written permission from the publisher, except in the case of brief quotations embodied in critical articles and reviews.

ACKNOWLEDGMENTS

The poem "Helpless" was first published online by *River Mouth Review* in January 2021.

The poem "To My Bystanders" was published by *River, Blood, and Corn* in March 2022.

Special thanks: to early readers, Claire Raines, Mary Holt, and Peggy Lore; to Suzi Q. Smith for generative prompts and generosity of spirit; to Kimberly L. Becker, for strong mentorship and more; to friends in the community who care and encourage; to familiar strangers who find their way to these pages; to my family, whose heart dwells within, behind, and between these lines; to life, in all its manifestations.

Publisher: Leah Huete de Maines
Editor: Christen Kincaid
Cover Art: Tightrope, zinc etching by Grant R. Williams,
      www.grantness.com
Author: Deborah Jang
Cover Design: Elizabeth Maines McCleavy

Order online: www.finishinglinepress.com
    also available on amazon.com and bookshop.org

Author inquiries and mail orders:
Finishing Line Press
PO Box 1626
Georgetown, Kentucky 40324
USA

Table of Contents

Metrics of neighborly friendship 1

Fade 2

Helpless 3

Stovetop meditation 5

Aging in place: a pep talk 6

Humblesong 8

Cloudscape 9

How to deep chat 10

Insomnia 11

Alien nation 13

Ode to yellow 14

To my bystanders 15

Moon juice 16

Forage 17

Rules of my wild 18

Bragging rights 19

Madness 20

Once upon another time 21

Fatherland 22

Holding 24

Of lambs and leopards 25

Germ pool getaway 27

A perfect death 30

Hereby 31

Last will and best guesses 32

The gratitudes 34

Metrics of neighborly friendship

Welcome here. The tomatoes
are plumping, drooping the vine.
They burst into their calling.
Swollen round and meaty,
the lusty vim, the eloquence,
bloating from within.

The yield offers plenty. Enough
to nourish anyone whose eyes
adrift come to rest, hushed upon
the fresh picked truth
of juicy homegrown tender.
Let them settle. Taste the splendor.
Let it dribble down your chin.

Gather now, linger among friends
and strangers. Lock eyes
with the neighbors. Knock elbows,
bend in not too far but close
enough to hum along
with hearts ripe and heavy.
Everyone, dig in.

Fade

I'm practically an ancestor—
One foot in the shallows,
the other salty deep.
Yellowed pearly wisdoms.
Sinew stretched past spry.
A barnacled demeanor.
A head of greying whispers.
A lifetime strewn on the path
to who knows where or why.
Sand bags stowed
beneath the eyes
hold remnants of the sorrow.
Tomorrow is no guarantee.
Children singing
make me weep.
As does the clarity of sky.
And all that shines
bejeweled beneath.

Helpless

Today in the pandemic
I folded paper cranes.

It's something I know how to do
when not much else makes sense
or seems to really matter.

Choose a pretty paper.
Match corners, each to each,
precisely and just so.
Press hard along the fold line
like there's no tomorrow.
Once more for good measure.

Today in the pandemic
I folded paper cranes.

For front line heroes geared up
in not much more
than their brave care
for the sick and dying.

Valley fold, straight and
clean along diagonal.
Then half as much
lengthwise again, repeat
now on the other side.
Turn inside corners up and out.
Thank them for their service.

Today in the pandemic
I folded paper cranes.

It all came back:
where to tuck, how to
finesse the paper bird,
where to pinch and gather.
I noticed that the
folding hands had grown
old and tattered. Yet deft

from years of hoping.

This is where we
mountain fold. Go for
crisp pointed corners.
(Perfection overrated.)
Paper magic in the palm
of your hand. Spread wings
gently outward.

Repeat.

Stovetop meditation

Low growing chatter, run-up to boil.
Just below surface, a loudening churn.
Steeped deep center, warm mist rises,
eyes and air soften. Mystery shows.

I watch pots for signs and wonders
when covid skies go cold.
Should tea leaves speak I'd bend
to listen, everyday I pray for wisdom

at stovetop altar now full roil.
Sacred cauldron—bubble, bubble.
Tending fire, blast of ages.
Quiet rapture. Ancient smolder.

Aging in place: a pep talk

Another morning rolls over,
outstretched and achy.
Memory dawns
on this strange familiar.

The sock drawer is now
the mask drawer. Death rattles
and ramps up its toll.

Tucked safe in a haven
—weathered and warm—
day upon day drones survival.

Blessings are counted with care.

Windows look out on a world wary.
Bright skies pour back in.
Sunshafts reveal
new old white hairs,
a neck kind of warbled and thin,
a brow grooved with worry,
grief deep in sockets
brim over pockets
of kindred despair.

The heart beats itself down.
The left hip complains.
The will a bit shaky but true.

Chop wood (metaphoric).
Get up (tragicomic).
Carry on, as grownups do.

Sign up, get your shots.
One more for good measure.
Grimace and gather,
each wherewithal matters.

Venture out on a limb
if you dare.

Walk, trot, or run—limp if you must—
towards the warm patter
of little feet roaming the hall.

Tend the chapped parts
of a world breaking. Numbers still
bleak, still trending.

Let brittle bones clatter.
Let muscles flame.
Offer what's left of flesh-
encased days breathing out mantras
that keep old hearts repeating ...

Humblesong

Tucked below the treble clef,
metered to the rising chest,
as once fresh and eager eyed
succumb to self-inflicted sighs
and happy ever afters die.

That promise never given.

Sassy tones and told you so's
lose resonance and vigor.

Might rings less triumphant here,
droned deep within the minor chords
along toe-dragging rhythms.

In and out repeating lines,
each iteration more sublime
bows to life's persistent thrum.

Humbled or humiliated, check
hubris at the temple door.

Find right pitch. Open throat.
Intone. Bend and enter.

Cloudscape

Whale. Dog. Bunny.
Penguin. Dragon. Moose.
Monkey on a mountain.
Three-legged bull.
Dissipating triceratops.
Texas upside down.
The continent of Africa.

A white gull screeches through.

Billowing commotion.
Drifting nonchalance.
Puffs of effervescence.
Dreams fending for themselves.
Playground of lost angels.
Cotton candy nothingness.
The aftertaste of Gone.

I often wonder about you.

Stray strands upon horizon
gather on a breeze.
Vague yet volatile.
Witness from beyond.
Infinite shapeshifters.
Vapors of unknowing.
Ghosts of silent elsewheres.

Flame consumed in blue.

How to deep chat

Start eye to eye with plain hellos.
Move to simple candor.
Open heart, reach way in.
Find a way beyond squirm.
Turn your insides outward.
Avoid the bragging banter.

Test your truth in whispers.
Let memory grow stronger.
Speak of things that matter most.
The history of happiness.
How to mend the broken fence.
The wound behind the rage.

Dredge up songs of redress
for lifetimes overcome.
Sing along and softly.
You might find smooth harmony.
You might hear lost melody
bursting out the seams.

Drink to the brink of despair.
Brim eyes with salt and citrus.
Share dashed hopes, dregs of dreams.
Let particulars spill over.
Curb the silent judgment.
Listen without measure.

Let night descend deep, then deeper.
Raise glasses high to moon.
Watch dawn rise on tomorrow.
Reconsider where you end.
Swallow one another's pride.
Polish off surrender.

Insomnia

Night tucks her in and blankets over.
Cups her forehead at the sweet spot.
Drifts off to crickets,
leaving her face upward,
staring into lifetimes.

While others slip rhythmic
into their far flung stories,
droning into escapades
that amuse us in the morning—
she breathes at bay the bogeyman

Who nibbles around her edges
like waves chomping on the shore,
obsessed, it seems,
with persistent schemes
of drama and annoyance.

She makes lists in her mind in the dark
even though she is not a list maker.

She recites her latest greatest
and realizes there are miles
to go before great
ness.

Gets up and wanders nighttime.
Resists the belly growling.
Wanting
Needing
Pleading with the sandman.

Plugs pods into her ears,
desperate for the wisdom,
secrets of the sages,
mysteries of nightime.

The sheep are not yet helping—
half hearted leaps and

baas and bleats fade
to grainy chatter
abuzz inside the head.

The meditation itches.
Memory unhinges.
Paranoia stalks with restlessness and vigor.

Surrender then. No matter.
Let the sleepless gather
beyond midnight graces.
Breathe in long, ease out slow.
Repeat. Repeat. Now let go.

Now go to
                sleep   now
float
float true
       and
              further …
Baaa
                                      blah, yes indeeeeeeed,
sirrrrrrrr
                      three
                                bags

       full.

Alien nation

Dark-eyed stranger.
Bright busy world.

Cacophonies and whirligigs.
Dazzling rapidities.

Voices deep that hem then haw.
Teams triumphant holler.

Looking on, she peers about,
out far corners of each eye.

Winces at the heavy hand,
the mad dash, the golden prize,

The scramble and its aftermath,
Plans and schemes, reinvestments,

A planet spinning off its axis,
People pushing at their process.

Silent, stray, she plays along,
Smiles some then moves on.

Ode to yellow

Yer from the yellow race, aintcha?
The whiskered man at the feed store
seemed proud of his perception.

A box to neatly put me in.
A color-coded novelty.
Othered in our difference.
Set aside for reference.
Or generally ignored.

Or treated as an enemy.
We, the yellow peril.

Or denounced repeatedly
as global viral blame.

Autumn bursts bright yellow.
Splendor screams.
Vibrance keens.

An earnest pigmentation
preceding winter's bleak.

Quaking aspen
Honey locust
River birch
Beech
Me

Fellow yellow hangers on.

Hello, world.
We're here.

To my bystanders

> *People stand by during attack of elderly Asian woman*
> —*Associated Press*

Did you catch a whiff of lilac
on that warm summer eve
while we gathered at the bus stop,
each wandering our mind?

Out the corner of your eye
did you flinch, did you see him
rushing twilight, pushing rudely in?

In a flash of recognition,
did your stomach tell your throat
what was going down?

Did you see my toes curl fetal
while I lay sideways
on the concrete stunned?

Did you freeze in fear and horror?
Did you look the other way?
Did you reach down for your phone
or was it already in your hand?

Were you scared to intervene?
Did your silence cheer him on?

Was it you who kneeled down
and whispered something kind
I didn't understand?

Did you see my bruised face on TV?
Did they say my name?
Did they even try?

Moon juice

Low tide spreads a welcome mat.
Shoreline widens.
Shyly beckons.

Devotees scan ocean floor—
Tread soft among small twisted temples
scattered upon holy ground.

Press shell to ear's grooved gristle,
A rush of quiet, here.

Swirled smooth along
the channeled edge,
descend each hidden chamber.

Breathe into the secret, where
pearlescent passageways
turn upon the golden axis
spiraling to bone,

ensconcing grace
in toned translucence,

deep space warmed in sand.

Dwell sloe eyed and full frontal.
Uncurated for good favor,
Unseen in one's prime.

Lost to time and measure,
tuck into the hallowed nub,
the innermost of what it is,
or was, or will ever be.

Never less nor more than.
Anointed from within.

Down here in the down low.
Settle into whole.

Forage

Pause a moment at the brink,
drawing deep the belly breath.
Between the cracks where
lost things go, uncharted ground
spreads before.

Enter there unscripted.
Rucksack empty
but for notions of kindness.
You could strew breadcrumbs
back to your own shabby shelter,
wind-battered as it is last standing.

Or rather wander tree to strong tree
foraging green mysteries,
steadying your raspy rhythms
so as not to disturb bogs and marshes
brewing life in shafts of sunlight
and cool shadow.

Should you perceive a presence there,
a familiar stranger, you
might dare let yourself be seen,
behold, be held in gazes—
long, arrested, mirrored.

That strip you of excuses
down to your hallowed skin.
That dress your wounds
with the sweet balm of recognition,

Quieting your feet upon a land
whose roots, entwined, entangled,
now release. Returning you
to your own true wild where—
unnamed, unclaimed—you
have always and only belonged.

Rules of my wild

1. Speak if you want, or not, without strain or fever.

2. If not, then snuggle up with silence. Curl into its sundry folds. Wrap yourself in white flags.

3. Exercise your heart daily: climb a hill or cry.

4. Warm in heaven's radiance, a slow flush from mid-core, welling to a gritty hallelujah.

5. During a pandemic, isolate the fear.

6. Take refuge under the guardian oak. Press back against its broadside. Wait for air to ripple.

7. Stay spacious. Be gracious.

8. Smile, for no one but your truest self. Let lips stretch and widen til your eyes become new moons.

9. Attend the broken dream. Hand heart to hope. Hold on.

10. To maintain equilibrium, sway like sea grass dancing in the underflow. If someone taps you on the shoulder, open your face fully their way.

11. Wash one another's feet. Sing or hum while doing so.

12. Let your heart be broken into one thousand sorrows. Greet sadness like that faithful guest, quietly returning.

13. Explode in laughter on occasion. Be the giggle.

14. Find a toddler or two. Get down on the floor and play.

15. Get down on the floor and pray. Don't close your eyes. Just breathe.

Bragging rights

I excel at giving the evil eye.
More than once I've been told
I can throw spears with a look, I'm told.

I suppose it is my secret power,
like the Incredible Hulk
and his green hulky glower.

It just happens sometimes,
a spontaneous scowl from deep within
when I feel wronged or disrespected
or as I witness such treatment
upon sisters and brothers.

But more than a scowl,
a shaft of disgust, shoots straight
out my eye into the soul
of the unsuspecting offender—

Who with one glance dismissed me as mild,
who mistook the silence of one broken child,
who has little regard for elders or women
or any human darker than him.

I dish it right back. I make them sweat.
Voodoo eyes burn through the bullshit
of their desperate hour.

I hope none of you ever get caught
in the terrible path of my hard-driven frown
that shrivels the balls of small sorry minds,

It seethes right through their lethal pride,
pierces their shame, inspires regret,
makes them squirm under the gaze
where grown men cower.

Madness

My anger's like a sleeping dog
deep in REM-cycled twitches.
Trembling under thin skinned lids
worlds churn beneath the surface.
Reflexive legs stir the air
on long journeys and far fetches.
Panting soft in strange quick fits.
Lip smacking high-pitched whimpers.
Potential snarls snuffle into
slobbers and furred secrets.
Do not disturb the matted splay,
pink tender belly rising.
Let it lie, the sleeping dog.
Let's pray it never wakens.

Once upon another time

My mom bet my dad I would be born
on his birthday, October 13, a Friday.
That afternoon she mowed the lawn hard
to make it come true: She got her wish.
He got his gift. I got his flat feet
and her brand of humor.

Sometimes things end, she explained.
We falter and bend. One morning
he paused at the cracked leather sofa on his way
to the door. We winced as it opened,
daylight flooded in upon three pairs of eyes
watching him go. His silhouette sagged and faded.

I've never seen him cry like that,
my mom confided later. Memory blurs.
It was a sloppy goodbye. A slobbering kiss
that left my face wet. Or were those his tears
that I felt? Or maybe mine? I don't know.

But this I discovered through years that followed.
The seeds of survival run sweet, run sour.
Some parents stay, rough in the tumble,
fighting new demons in between wisps
of tender affection. She tried so hard
to make happily ever ...

After all has been offered, goodbyes
completed, what remains long after
salt stained ocean sprinklings
a lifetime yet traces—faces
drying in soft breezes forever.
Love is what's left after the leaving.

Fatherland

The neat square of his thumbnail.
Front teeth to match and gleam.
Glee could burst his face wide open.
Laughter jiggled belly free.

He painted pictures on the wall.
Built a houseboat made of junk.
On Sundays bought glazed donuts.
Walked us to the nearby park,
rolled us down the hill.

Old photos show him horn rimmed,
crew cut. Then the shaggy sixties,
then next decade's frizzy perm.
A man of and for the changing times
until time set him free.

Up and down Route 99, singing,
oleander graced the way.
One parent, three children,
alternate weekends,
a whole month in the summer.

New wife and her son Teddy
turned kin in just a day.
Eyes stared across the nubby couch.
First one to break a smile lost.
Not me. Until eventually.

He opened shops of women's clothes.
Coached models how to runway walk
*As if a lemon's squeezed between
your lovely knees. Keep tight, that's right.*

Tassled fez atop his head
bobbed with singing vigor.
One of boys, fraternal joy.
*Oklahoma! Yankee Doodle.
Stars and Stripes Forever.*

Then later, in his weathered chair,
taste morsels from the old country—
lychee, pigs feet, smoked abalone.
Sprinkled with a dash of bitters,
Downed with whisky sours.

Holding

The past but a puzzle of forgotten best efforts.
Makeshift scraps of stray memory.
A dozen soft donuts glazed mornings after
nighttimes imploded just down the hall.

A marching band practiced across the street.
My dad let us draw on our bedroom wall.
Creeks and canals were things not to fall into.
The smell and sizzle of bacon was strong.

When moving day came, we traded daddies.
Homes rearranged, kin subdivided.
We found the cat, she was having more kittens.
We were welcomed with taunts, and run from.

We were welcomed with pie served on a bible.
I bit, believing their smiles could save me.
I sit, now a beggar, a bowl full of nothing
but a strawberry moon that holds, round and long.

Of lambs and leopards

I found Jesus in the neighbors' backyard.
He lived in my heart for a spell.
I decided to get baptized and join the church flock.
I walked forward to let them know.

Lamb of God, I come, I come.
I went, I went. I whispered why.
The church folk smiled
in tune with the organ.
The music swallowed me whole.

As the moment of truth drew near,
I invited my mom to attend.
She donned her leopard-spotted pillbox hat
because you always wear a hat to church,
she, the Episcopalian, claimed.
It was her first visit to Calvary Baptist—
immersion and bare heads preferred.

Up front in the spotlight, water to knees,
I professed, took a breath.
The pastor dunked me under.
I sputtered up, knowing she was out there
in her leopard-spotted pillbox hat.
I beamed in my wet hair.

I wondered if she sang along.
I wondered if the spirit moved her.
She kept her thoughts tucked under her hat
as she drove the soggy lamb home.

Some years later we sat and drank
our first glass of wine together.
I forget the occasion. I think it was red.
Paired with a cheese.
She the experienced drinker.

Clink clink went glass lips. I took a sip.
The taste was sweet, slightly sour.
My cheeks turned warm then rosy.

A cozy feeling spread.
Flushed in the moment,
her cigarette glowing,
I noticed how much I loved her.

Years after that she confessed
her relief at our wine precedent,
for my piety had concerned her.
I realized then we had been
to each a reciprocal blessing.
She a witness to my dunking.
My immersion into her drink—
mutual holy communions.
Sanctified payback. Amen.

Germ pool getaway

You have driven for hours,
me riding shotgun,
feet rude on the dash,
toes toasting each other
in the windshield's warmth.

We pass chugging truckers
looking down from their thrones,
bulldogs of the interstate—
at least the right lanes—taking
it in from their perches on high.

From six mighty lanes we merge
into four. One each for passing
either direction. The center line
squirms. The road wiggly
and worn.

Outsiders, we roll through
dusty downtowns.
Past old movie houses,
streets full of locals living their lives,
staring at us.

Old billboards speak volumes
now silent and battered.
Skeletal structures once
bright with enticement—
now tattered temples of time.

At mile marker 40 we get in a fight
over some silly matter.
At the next rest stop
cool off over sausages
pouting in buns. The mustard
is spicy, nobody wins.

Next day begins early
with coffee, ice water, and chips,
why not? Roadside attractions

do not distract us from urgent notions
of forward momentum.

You wrestle the map while
I roll my eyes and consult
the device for precise
navigation. *Speak up, I can't
hear you.* AT THE NEXT EXIT
VEER GENTLY RIGHT.

This state is a sculpture.
It draws us in among mounds,
sandstone hollows, craggy steep peaks—
Like ants we crawl steady through
awesome dimension.

Haystacks look tired, sagging
in fields, crisped under sun's blaze.
Loitering bundles rolled
or rectangled, stacked against sky.
Monet would revive them.

Silence is comfy, long stretches
needed to let minds flow easy,
filtering scenes through
vague memories suddenly keen.
Remember the time we made love
on those rocks?

Two nights of camping—max—
before hot shower needed.
Sweet spot by the river
brings it all home. Campfire magic.
Milky Way dome. Rocky formations
impress and inspire.
Not bad for old codgers
dodging a virus.

Miles behind us, more ahead
if we're lucky. It is a fine

journey with you beside me.
Who ever knows when this road
will peter. Until then, let us ramble
on towards land's end. Thanks
for the ride.

A perfect death

When I die, let it not be a scene
of tragic nor dramatic portions.
No headline making horror show—
not the granny pushed and battered,
not one among a massive murder,
nor victim x of a serial killer,
nor alone on ventilator.

May it be a peaceful leaving,
Nighttime's tiptoed undertaking.
Or in tender consciousness,
tucked between the waning breaths.
May last goodbyes all be spoken,
one by one, no regrets.

With dignity may I go gentle.
May hair fall neatly and just right.
No lingering excruciation.
No false hoping for survival.
No denying. Face full forward
like the moon—steady, knowing.
Keep me warm. Hold me tight.

Escorted by the mystery
beyond humanity's long plight
into realms uncomprehended,
onward with the best of them.
Letting go a lifetime's measure,
at rest at last—breath's nothingness.
Nothing more, nothing less.

Hereby

Of sound mind and body whole,
In perpetuity,
for now,

Hereby stuttered out
in whispers
lest the Sorrows overbear,

For too many rudely taken
by disease, neglect, or gun,

Through this passage
of brute blunder,

absence riddles endless seasons.

Here the moment
meets the mortal—
while body bags line freezer trucks,

At the brink of all that matters,
By the twilight let us gather
either side of the river,

Tangle tears
by cool waters,

Walk among them.

Wash the feet of heroes fallen,
Dry the eyes of caged children,
Bend a knee for lifetimes shattered,

Muffled,
howling hoarse to heaven,

Clutching earth, changed forever.

Last will and best guesses

To you who take to
soul-bared scribbles
spread eagle on cool pages,

To you whose ears hum
up the brain stem at finger popping
nitty-gritty, ushered out
prophetic mouths, resounding
mind to mind,

To you who tend to wander lost
in aftermaths and ruminations,

To you who cringe at mystery,
To you who tolerated me,
To you who walked on by—

I leave a sack of syllables,
chewed on and delivered,
sitting at your doorstep basking
soft in sun,

I leave words unspoken,
boatloads brimming in the bay,
not for lack of caring
but like the shy and shiny wish
before you blow the candles out,

I leave a fading shadow, a shuffled
footprint, a trinket here and there,
nothing much to speak of
in the way of fortune's matter,

I leave you to the truth of you
lodged deep, let it roar,

I leave configurations,
dimensions of hand and heart
and time slowed, flowing
through creation,

I leave regrets. Please bury them
at the bottom of the sea,
where they can feed
on the dregs of possibility,
barnacled and broken,
rising free from yesterdays,

If and when you think of me
I am best digested settled
into cozy corners. Let the sun
glance off your shoulder.
Let whatever words attend you
meet the wild woe.

I leave you, gently so.

The gratitudes

Waking to the robin's trill
summoning first light.

Plus distant hoot of mourning dove.
Plus this air, its cool refresh.
Plus the creep of consciousness.

Blanketed in solitude,
nestled deep within the folds,

To the beat where hope abides,
hope by hope by hope, arise.
Make way to the epicenter
of each moment's full imbue.

There, let flow the Gratitudes—

For snug embrace of this place
where mind settles into heart,
free from urgent expectation.
Dwell. Forgive. Repair. Repeat.

For the grandeur of small feet,
the funny words, the finest pouts,

For beloved, grubby faces,
thank you for these wonder years.

For this supple earthenware,
strong enough to devour
every welcomed blast of warmth,
For radiance against this skin,
for melanin, its knowing tones.

For kin of every ilk and bearing,
For reconnection bone by bone,

For the pounding of the surf,
for ocean spray, the salty breath,

For tastes and textures from far corners
partying upon the tongue,

For music of the inner sanctum
rising to a glory beat,

For another chance to dance,
romance the light from east to west,
incite the mind, bend the hour.

For wanderers who wandered in,
sat and chatted, fast became
sturdy and forgiving friends—
Thank you for the ones who stayed.

For the strong and brilliant, resilient
and faithful keepers of the light,
thank you for insightful caring.

For kind touch, the goodnight kiss.
After each delight or drama,
for the concert of our laughter.

For yet another day's survival
in a world where land mines lurk
underneath the unsuspecting.
Please and thank you for protection.

Thank you for the afterglow,
For the stars to steer by,
For truth that hits between the eyes.
For memory, what's left of it,
that takes us deeper deeper.

For second chances, third, and fourth,
fifth and sixth, ad infinitum
as long as breath still fogs the mirror.

And when it stops, for having known
life in its configurations,
Mind bent, nose blown, fingers crossed.
Head bowed, going home.

Deborah Jang maintains both a writing and a visual arts practice as a means of processing her place in, and probing the permutations of, the world at large as well as at its most intimate. She is based in Denver, Colorado, and Oceanside, California. Her sculptural work has been shown across the U.S., and can be found in corporate and private collections, as well as in various community settings. Her debut book of poetry, *Float True,* was published in March 2020.

www.ingramcontent.com/pod-product-compliance
Lightning Source LLC
LaVergne TN
LVHW041555070426
835507LV00011B/1105